IRAN'S GREAT INVASION
AND WHY IT'S NEXT IN BIBLE PROPHECY

MARK DAVIDSON

WESTBOW
PRESS®
A DIVISION OF THOMAS NELSON
& ZONDERVAN

This is a work of fiction. All of the characters, names, incidents, organizations, and dialogue
in this novel are either the products of the author's imagination or are used fictitiously.

WestBow Press books may be ordered through booksellers or by contacting:

WestBow Press
A Division of Thomas Nelson & Zondervan
1663 Liberty Drive
Bloomington, IN 47403
www.westbowpress.com
1 (866) 928-1240

Cover created by www.charityleblanc.com.

ISBN: 978-1-5127-7538-9 (sc)
ISBN: 978-1-5127-7537-2 (e)

Library of Congress Control Number: 2017902130

Print information available on the last page.

WestBow Press rev. date: 12/15/2017

ENDORSEMENTS

We are quickly approaching the time where "realities on the ground" will force people to reconsider Bible prophecy. The coming Iranian invasion of the Middle East will do just that. What Mark has done is create a very quick read for those Christians who can feel something coming, but can't put their finger on it; who know that God is in control, but in a world spiraling into chaos, don't know where to go scripturally. I believe this will also provide a "lifeline" to non-Christians who know they are missing something and will look to an ancient book and an omniscient God for answers. As the pastor in this story does, many will have to reevaluate their understanding of Daniel 8 . . . and fast. Hand this book out to all you can.

—**Christopher Mantei**,
Managing director, WingsOfTheEagle.com, and
Northeast Region Community
Voice, Voice of the Martyrs

In 2014, I ordered a book by Mark Davidson, entitled *Daniel Revisited,* that transformed my thinking and theology regarding Daniel's visions in the biblical book of Daniel. I had always taught a revived and revised Roman Empire that would arise in the last days, with a European Antichrist. After reading Mark's book, I realized the last days' empire is going to be Islamic, with an Islamic Antichrist.

Now Mark has written a short version entitled *Iran's Great Invasion* that describes the soon-coming Iranian invasion of the Middle East. He says, "The next great prophetic event is not the rapture, but a Sunni/Shia war that will affect not only the Middle East, but the nations of the world." If you want to know the truth regarding present-day events in the Middle East, and how they will affect you and your family, you need to get the book. A major fire has been lit and few are paying attention.

—**Dr. W. L. "Sonny" Payne,**
Founder and president of New Gate Ministries, author of the book *The DNA of Jesus Christ*, and host of the international television program, *Jerusalem Chronicles.*

I'm excited and encouraged to highly recommend a compelling book that is biblical, insightful, provocative, and hopeful as we speed rapidly into the mystery of the future. Mark Davidson's book, *Iran's Great Invasion and Why It's Next in Bible Prophecy,* takes a deep and careful look at passages in the book of Daniel and how they line up with the events in the Middle East happening today.

Written as a story, this is a quick and enlightening read as Davidson prepares us for the next events to happen on God's timetable. My mind was captured and my heart was warmed with the powerful combination of biblical truth measured with all the fascinating and troubling developments that are taking place in the world today.

The message in this book needs to be heard today! I wholeheartedly and enthusiastically recommend this book. It will change the way you face the future!

—**Carl Sutter,**
Senior and founding pastor, Foundations Church, Loveland, CO

CONTENTS

ACKNOWLEDGMENTS

My thanks go to the readers of *Daniel Revisited*, the brothers and sisters who are now partnering with me in the work of declaring this new end-time message to the churches. I am grateful they made it clear to me this book was needed, with its message geared for all the people in their lives who are not prophecy students, spelling out the warning regarding Iran's invasion of the Middle East. Their support made this book a reality.

What you are about to read is presented in the form of a story,
but the subject matter is real and fully presented
in *Daniel Revisited* by Mark Davidson.
The story is based on dozens of conversations the author has had
with pastors and ministry leaders
concerning the message of this book.

PROLOGUE

What would *you* do?

What if you stumbled across a message, a simple interpretation of Scripture—much simpler than scholars had been telling us—and it opened your eyes and completely transformed your perspective of the end times? You knew in your heart and mind it was true, because news events coming from the Middle East confirmed this message every day.

What if this message showed that the Rapture was not next, nor the Tribulation, but rather some terrible events triggering several years of very hard times affecting the entire world—events that would shake the foundations of your faith, as well as that of the whole church?

What if the message was also a dire warning to watch for, and get ready for, the second coming of Jesus?

What if millions of lives were about to be deeply affected, and someone had to say something? And what if that someone had to be you?

What would you *do*?

Would you reach out to everyone in the church that you could and risk being called a kook? Would you feel a moral imperative to warn unsuspecting Christians? Would you just sit on the message and do nothing? Would you do what the Holy Spirit, and your conscience, was telling you to do?

What is this message? It is the message of the real end times. For years, the world and the church have witnessed Iran getting ready—for something. Only those believers who know the message can see what is coming. And what is coming will cause economic chaos and change the way we live our lives.

Iran is about to invade the Middle East. That nation will be used by God to set events in motion that will end years later with the Antichrist coming to power.

This will be the second most important message in the world when the events it predicts come to pass. This second most important message will allow those who spread the most important message—the gospel of Jesus Christ—to keep doing so calmly, providing answers to the lost, about salvation and the terrible things going on around them. They will know from God's Word what is really happening, while chaos grips the world.

Christ is coming, and time is short! It is time to wake up!

ONE

A VISIT

There it was. His destination was in sight—the large church building standing by the side of the road. Behind it was the office of the pastor with whom Mike Branch was scheduled to meet. It had been a long drive, so stopping to refill the gas tank seemed prudent.

The building was large and square, painted all white, with paned windows that seemed too small, and a tower. The church looked like the builders couldn't decide whether the style should be traditional with ascending roof, steeple, and stained glass, or boxy and contemporary, with no windows, as if a nightclub were inside.

Fittingly, the church seemed representative of the greater church, steeped in tradition but attempting to reach out to be relevant to society today. The road it stood by was a major thoroughfare of the city, with traffic speeding by. *Is this scene symbolic of the way most people are these days—too busy to stop to know their Lord, to allow Jesus Christ to reign in their hearts? He is coming soon, though the next sign of his coming is sooner than many may realize.*

It occurred to Mike that this was an appropriate place to share his urgent message—at this building that seemed to embody American Christianity both in its traditional and contemporary flavors. The pastors and congregation stood ready to receive all from the local populace who cared to hear about salvation through Jesus Christ. It stood ready to preach the gospel and lead the lost to Christ. This message would help it in the times soon to come as it was meant to—the real end times that God had disclosed in his Word two-and-a-half-millennia before.

Mike Branch's message was a new interpretation of an old prophecy. Derived from the plain and simple words in the text of the prophecy in Daniel—the words had been up to then mostly ignored. This wasn't too surprising, for the text of the prophecy itself said it was sealed until the end time. *This is the end time*, Mike thought, *and God's Word wouldn't say such a thing for nothing.*

He felt the usual twinge of anxiety when he shared this new prophetic message. It was hard to go against eighteen centuries of tradition, even if that tradition was based on guesses. To him, it seemed so simple and eye-opening, yet typically, nine out of ten pastors rejected it. It was rejected not because it went against what the Bible said, but because it went against the tradition they had been taught. The nine rejected it without even hearing it. *They are the ones who are going to wake up only when the great Iranian invasion is underway.*

Pastor Joe Taylor had a reputation of being a pillar of the Christian community in the city. Head of a Bible-teaching church, he had his own radio ministry, and even hosted a prophecy conference occasionally. He would certainly be well versed in what was popularly being taught about Bible prophecy.

As he pulled up into a space in the parking lot next to the pastor's office, Mike thought, *Glad I could get a meeting scheduled with him.* It was the end of the work week and the pastor's assistant had said the meeting was open ended. *Hope we'll have a meaningful discussion.* He knew how influential Taylor was, both in the church and in the community. Rich, a mutual friend, had set the meeting up, telling the pastor his friend had an urgent message, a new interpretation with a relevant warning for the days ahead.

The churches are asleep, he thought, as he walked across the parking lot. Like the virgins of Matthew 25, the churches were asleep to what was soon to come in the end times—dozing and comfortable with whatever they thought was next—the Rapture, the Second Coming, or even the Nephilim. But a shocking awakening was coming, and it was all revealed by the simple words in Daniel. The true next event was something sinister. But Daniel had also said the vision would be sealed until the time of the end, so how could anyone have known?

He prayed, "Lord put the right words in my mouth, and let Pastor Taylor be receptive."

As Mike entered through a door in the back of the church, Sharon, the pastor's assistant greeted him and ushered him in to the pastor's spacious office saying, "Pastor, Mike Branch is here to see you."

"Pastor Taylor, it's good to meet you," Mike said as the two men shook hands. "Thank you for seeing me."

"My pleasure; nice to meet you." He gestured toward a round table with several chairs placed around it. After they were seated and had chatted a bit, Pastor Taylor said, "By the way, Mike, please call me Joe. Our friend, Richard, said you wanted to share a new end-time message with me. He seemed really excited about it. Said something about it being a warning we need to keep in mind."

"That's right. You might be shocked or surprised at some points building up to the conclusion—many have been—but if you can stay with me to the end, it should be eye-opening. You may find it valuable in the times to come."

"Sounds good. To be honest, the timing is interesting here. For the last few months, ever since I got back from our tour of Israel, I guess, I've been thinking about the end times. Feeling there is something more . . . something we've been missing. So, I'm anxious to hear what you have to say. Let's get started."

"That's indeed interesting," responded Mike, taking a deep breath. "This message presents a picture of the end times very different from what we thought. We *have* been missing something, and it all comes from ignoring some simple verses in prophecy about the end times."

"Go on . . ."

TWO

————◆◆×◆◆————

THE NEXT EVENT

"First," Mike said, leaning forward, "the next event to come in the fulfillment of end-time Bible prophecy is not the Rapture or the Tribulation."

"The Rapture isn't next?" Joe responded quickly, eyes wide and eyebrows raised. "Are you saying the Rapture is mid-Trib or perhaps even post-Trib or pre-Wrath?

"Well, that's a problem right there. I can tell you right now that both I and much of my church believe in a pre-Trib Rapture. We could argue all day about the timing of the Rapture so such a discussion would be pointless."

Mike could tell from slight shifts in the pastor's body language Joe might be thinking the discussion was already over.

"Understood," Mike said. "But I'm not saying that. I *am* saying, neither the Rapture nor the Tribulation is next. The Rapture, Tribulation, and their timing with respect to each other are irrelevant to this message. And just so we are clear, when we talk about the Tribulation, we are talking about the last seven years prior to Christ's return."

"Agreed."

Mike continued, "This new interpretation of Daniel points to a series of events that occur prior to both the Tribulation and the Rapture. So, whether the Rapture is pre-, mid-, or post-Trib, or even pre-Wrath, it doesn't matter. Not only that, all of us have missed these next events. They are not even on the church's radar. Let me explain and I'll show you how this happened."

"You think the whole church has missed an event that is in the Bible?" The look on Joe's face wasn't one of acceptance.

"Yes, and actually not one event, but a series of events. This is usually the part of the message that shocks people—that some event is next and no one saw it coming." Mike shifted in his chair, and settled back before continuing. "It's due in part to theologians ignoring some verses in Daniel 8. Verses that, if interpreted literally, would change everything about our outlook on the end times. The church is expecting to be raptured. But this next event, if it occurs, will unleash economic chaos on the world leading up to the actual time of the Rapture or Tribulation. It will also unleash a terrible war in the Middle East on a scale that we have not seen in our lifetimes." Mike gestured to his black Bible on the table. "And it's all in the Bible."

He continued, "This chaos will cause people to panic and think the world is ending. The relative peace of mind we enjoy today—the ability of people to get to their jobs and provide a living for their families—will likely be taken away, to an extent, once the economic chaos kicks in. So that's why I'm here today to share this with you. Preachers and pastors must recognize what is happening, and that it was called out in God's Word. That way you can remain steady and calm, and continue your work of preaching the Gospel. Christians will need to have built their house on the rock, and all who teach the Bible need to have answers when this time comes."

"I'm listening," said Pastor Joe, his eyes firmly fixed on the other man. "Just what do you base this on?"

"The message comes from Daniel 8. A simple interpretation of Daniel 8 suggests Iran is going to invade most of the Middle East. Iranian forces will charge out from southwestern Iran, and take most of the Middle East, including all the oil fields. For a time, Iran will control one quarter of the world's oil production. When they do this, the Iranian regime will put an end to the US petrodollar. That'll cause economic chaos here in America and across much of the world."

"That's quite a claim."

"It's all there in Daniel 8. And it's implied in other places like Matthew and Revelation. But, I'm getting a little ahead of myself. Daniel 8 shows us the next prophetic event is Iran's invasion and occupation of the Middle East."

"So, when you say Daniel 8, that's the same chapter that tells us the vision of the ram and the goat?"

"That's right," Mike responded, "and we can go over it together, if you'd like."

"Yes, let's take a look. But wait, wasn't that fulfilled by the ancient Persian Empire and Alexander the Great? And wasn't the little horn Antiochus Epiphanes?"

"That's what we've all been taught. But this cannot be so, and I'll show you why. Actually, Daniel 8 is teaching us something completely different. What it has to say may turn out to have great application to today. You see, it's all because of three verses in Daniel 8 that have been glossed over by the theology taught today."

Again, Pastor Joe's eyebrows were raised. "Which three verses?"

"The first one is Daniel 8:17. That's where the angel Gabriel tells Daniel about the vision and he says, 'Understand that the vision concerns the time of the end.'"

"What? Is that in there?" the pastor said, his voice sounding as if he didn't believe it. He grabbed his Bible and leafed through it to Daniel 8. His expression seemed to show surprise mixed with a little annoyance. He spent a moment reading the verse silently.

"Huh. There it is. In my NKJV it says, 'Understand, son of man, that the vision refers to the time of the end.' I don't remember that verse being there, but there it is." Joe Taylor sat still, apparently thinking about what he had just read. "Hmm. I think I can also see why this verse has been ignored—it clashes with what we've always thought the prophecy means."

Mike responded, "Daniel 8 can't be fulfilled by the ancient Persian Empire if we take Daniel 8:17 literally. There's more," he said as he turned to his Bible. "Let's look at the second verse. You remember it says in Deuteronomy that a matter must be established by the testimony of two or three witnesses."

"And Jesus said that too, in Matthew 18:16," Joe added.

"That's right."

"Now go two verses past Daniel 8:17 to 8:19 and read that one."

Joe read out loud, "Look, I am making known to you what shall happen in the latter time of the indignation; for at the appointed time the end shall be." He looked thoughtful and said, "Hmm, *shall be*."

"In my NIV," Mike said, "It says, 'I am going to tell you what will happen later in the time of wrath, because the vision concerns the appointed time of the end.' The two versions are slightly different, but they say the same thing. The NIV is more direct, but the NKJV still says "the appointed time of the end." Why would it say that if the vision of Daniel 8 had anything to do with a fulfillment other than the 'time of the end'?"

"Admittedly, that's the second witness. But you said there are three verses?"

Just then, Sharon, Pastor Taylor's assistant came in and asked, "Can I get you something to drink?"

"Some bottled water, please, Sharon, and I'll have some tea. What would you like, Mike?"

Mike knew he would have a late night driving home so opted for coffee. Then the men got right back to the discussion.

"Yes, there's a third verse," Mike said. "But, before going on, we should look at why these verses have been skipped or ignored. The third verse actually touches on this subject."

"Hmm," Joe said, clearly interested.

"You mentioned the ancient Persian Empire. Back in the first century of the church, the Persian Empire's conquests and the appearance of Alexander the Great had just happened three centuries before. It was perfectly acceptable for the church fathers to assume Alexander was the goat in Daniel 8, and the Persian Empire was the ram, since those things had happened fairly recently. Christians in the first century believed they lived in the end times. So the interpretation of ancient Persia and Alexander seemed to fit at that time.

"But then the centuries rolled by. And here we are two thousand years later and we are still saying the ram is ancient Persia and the goat is Alexander the Great! Perhaps it's because respected church fathers first said it. Untold numbers of pastors and teachers have repeated it. So this interpretation regarding ancient Persia and Alexander the Great has been deemed untouchable, unquestionable."

Mike paused as if to let that sink in. "It's clear, since Daniel 8 pertains to the end times, it's time to question, to reexamine tradition. It's been twenty-three centuries since Alexander the Great."

Just then the pastor's assistant came in with a tray of the hot drinks and water, and a small plate of cookies, and set them on the table. "If you need something, let me know; I'll be working late tonight," she said before shutting the door behind her.

The men each grabbed a mug before Mike said, "So, now the third verse is Daniel 8:26. Go ahead and take a look."

The pastor read silently for a moment. Then he read out loud, "Therefore seal up the vision, for *it* refers to many days in the future."

Mike said, "My NIV reads, 'Seal up the vision, for it concerns the distant future.' Since Daniel wrote those words, about 2,500 years have elapsed. I wonder what would be 'distant future' to Daniel? Two centuries in the future to the time of Alexander the Great? Maybe twenty-five centuries in the future to our time? I believe 'distant future' is more likely our time than Alexander's time. That's three places now where Daniel 8 says the vision is to occur in the end time."

"I see that," said Joe thoughtfully, looking down at the verses. "The vision, too, would likely have one fulfillment. If verse 17 says the vision 'refers to the time of the end,' verse 19 says 'time of the indignation' and verse 26 says 'distant future' I would think at first glance all these phrases meant the same thing."

"Not only that," Mike said, "but do you see how Daniel 8:26 shows us *why* theologians kept repeating the same traditional interpretation about Alexander the Great and the ancient Persian Empire?"

As Joe scanned verse 26, Mike said, "The vision of Daniel 8 is sealed until the end time. Daniel 8:26 says so. Sealing a scroll means it cannot be read. You know, there's a place in Isaiah—Isaiah 29:11—where it talks about a prophecy to be given to the Jews, but it is written on a scroll and sealed. The verse says in my NIV Bible, 'For you this whole vision is nothing but words sealed in a scroll. And if you give the scroll to someone who can read, and say to him, 'Read this, please,' he will answer, 'I can't; it is sealed.'"

Joe was obviously mulling this over. "Hmm. So, not only does

Daniel 8 tell us in three places that the vision is in the end times, it's even telling us as well that we won't really wake up and understand the vision until we reach the end times. That's actually quite remarkable, if you think about it. It confirms yet again the Word of God itself is living."

"What's also remarkable to me," Mike responded, "Daniel 8 is not only telling us it's likely to be fulfilled in our time, but it looks as if it has already started being fulfilled. The signs of it are already all over Iran and the Middle East. I believe we are already seeing proof of the end-time fulfillment of Daniel 8!"

"What?" the pastor asked, his eyes widening.

"That's right. There is a verse toward the beginning of Daniel 8 revealing an event ahead of Iran's invasion. Something happens to the ram. And it looks like it has already happened. The problem is, it hasn't been reported in the mainstream media, but it has nevertheless happened."

Mike's voice grew more animated as he said, "We are practically at the door of the possible fulfillment of the main event of Daniel 8! The church has been asleep at the helm, so to speak. The centuries have slowly elapsed since ancient Persia and Alexander the Great. It should have become clear to anyone reading Daniel 8 literally, that any 'fulfillment' from the Persian Empire and Alexander wasn't possible anymore. What seemed like the end times to the ancients, ended up becoming ancient history to us. We're the ones who are really living in the end times!

"But, I think this is part of God's plan. Daniel 8:26 says God's plan is that the vision is misunderstood and the true meaning overlooked until the end time when it's supposed to happen! The vision of Daniel 8 was to be sealed until the end time. And so it has been until now! The three verses, 17, 19, and 26, have been ignored, and an outdated interpretation forced on Daniel 8."

"That's more than remarkable—it's amazing," answered Joe. "Huh. And word of this is only going out now?"

The Three Verses of Daniel 8
Showing the Vision Will Be Fulfilled in the End Times
(NIV 1984, emphasis added)

Daniel 8:17: "'Son of man,' he said to me, 'understand that the *vision concerns the time of the end.*'"

Daniel 8:19: "I am going to tell you what will happen later in the time of wrath, because the *vision concerns the appointed time of the end.*"

Daniel 8:26: "The vision of the evenings and mornings that has been given you is true, but *seal up the vision, for it concerns the distant future.*"

"Apparently," Mike said. "I came across a book called *Daniel Revisited* [1] by Mark Davidson. I read it just after it came out in early 2014. Haven't seen the message coming from anywhere else. When I couldn't get it off my mind, I started looking into the Scriptures for myself. I've been visiting pastors to share what I found out since then, as I really feel it's urgent."

"I was wondering how you came across this new interpretation. Looks like I'll have to read that book," Joe said, looking thoughtful. "OK, I can see how it's possible the fulfillment of the ram and goat could be anytime now due to those three verses. But you said it was next. How can you know that?"

"Good question. It's due to that verse toward the beginning of Daniel 8 I mentioned earlier. And we know it from the context of the vision in Daniel 8. Let's look at the whole vision."

The two men looked carefully at verses 3 to 12 in Daniel 8 in their Bibles. Then Mike Branch pulled a chart from the back of his Bible and laid it on the table. "Here's a chart listing the five parts the vision can be divided into.

The Five Parts of the Vision of the Ram and Goat

Part	Verses	Description of the Vision Parts
1	3	Ram's second horn grows.
2	4	Ram with two horns charges in three directions.
3	5–7	Goat with great horn runs east and attacks ram.
4	8-9	Four horns replace the one horn on the goat; little horn grows in power from one of four horns.
5	10–12	Grown horn makes war on the saints; ends daily sacrifice, during Tribulation.

"The invasion by Iran is in verse 4. But something else happens first in verse 3 which may have already happened. Let's first look at the whole vision."

Joe said, "In the traditional way of looking at Daniel 8, that last horn to grow in power in verse 9 and making war on the saints in verse 10 was attributed to the Greek king Antiochus Epiphanes."

"But with this vision occurring in the end times," said Mike, "This horn making war on the saints is not Antiochus Epiphanes but would be the Antichrist himself. There are only two figures mentioned in the Bible living after the time of Daniel who will stop the sacrifice—Antiochus and the Antichrist. Ending the sacrifice is mentioned in Daniel 8:11 and confirmed to be by the Antichrist in Daniel 9:27. This would be during the time of the Tribulation."

As the pastor looked down at the chart, Mike continued. "Now, if part 5 of the vision about the ending of the sacrifice is during the Tribulation, part 4 must be before that time—the time of the horn starting to grow. If the Antichrist makes or confirms a covenant with many at the start of the Tribulation, as it also says in Daniel 9:27, then at *that* time he is already in a position of power. So if it's prior to the Tribulation, part 4 in Daniel 8:9 is actually showing us the Antichrist growing in power. And it's coming from one of four new nations that appear and replace the first horn of the goat, also in part 4. In part 3, the goat attacks the ram. The goat will be a nation to the west of Iran—likely Turkey. This is all supposed to happen in the Middle East."

Joe said, "Well, all this brings another interesting twist to end-time prophecy."

"Let me guess what you might be thinking," responded Mike Branch, "the Antichrist?"

"Yes!" responded the pastor, his voice sounding excited at the prospect of a newly discovered find augmenting an old end-time topic. "Personally, I'm not married to any opinion on the Antichrist's origins. But, you know as well as I do that much of the Protestant church believes the Antichrist will come from Rome or at least Europe."

"I know," Mike said. "Yet, here we see Scripture giving us the case for the Antichrist actually coming from the Middle East, if this interpretation is true. Personally, I think that belief in a Roman Antichrist has only helped with the sealing of Daniel 8. Even if the ram and goat were seen all along to represent events leading to some great leader in the end times, there is no motivation to look deeper into Daniel 8. If the Antichrist comes from Europe, who would the last horn be in Daniel 8? Antiochus Epiphanes has been a convenient figure to attach to the little horn, which has probably helped to propagate the traditional view of Daniel 8. But now we can see Daniel 8 shows us the emergence of the Antichrist; the events prior to his appearance."

"Interesting," said Joe thoughtfully. "You know, everyone says the iron legs of the statue in Daniel 2 are Rome. Instead, it would have to be what, Islam? Can such a case be made?"

"Yes, it can. In fact, when you study the history of Rome and Islam, Islam shows itself a better candidate than Rome as the candidate of the iron-leg empire. It is impossible for Rome to be the candidate if one pays careful attention to the text of the verse, and compares the text with what actually happened in history.

"Daniel 2:40 says the empire of the iron legs has to crush or pulverize the other prior empires in the statue. This suggests that Babylon, Persia, and Greece all had to be *smashed* in terms of their language, religion, and culture. Regarding Greece, Rome was taken over by Greek culture. And Rome didn't even conquer Persia, so it never had the opportunity to break up or smash Persia. Islam, however, with its writings and ways, relentlessly, over centuries, changed the language and religion of almost everyone living in Babylon, Persia, and most of the areas that Alexander conquered. Today, only the country of Greece has survived centuries of Islamic occupation as a Christian nation.

"This is all made clear in Davidson's *Daniel Revisited*.[2] There's another author you should read, Joel Richardson. In *Mideast Beast,* he writes about this as well.[3]"

"But what do you do with Daniel 9:26 and the people of the ruler who will come?" inquired Joe. "How do you show they were not Romans?"

Mike sat back in his chair, and said, "In Daniel 9:26, the word for 'people' in that verse can mean political people or ethnic people. For example, the apostle Paul says in his letters that he is a Jew of the tribe of Benjamin. The book of Acts records he also says he is a Roman citizen. So we see in Paul an ethnic background and a political background. Several historical sources show us that the soldiers who destroyed Jerusalem in AD 70 were indeed fighting for Rome, and wearing Roman uniforms, but they were not Italians or even Europeans. They were Syrians, Egyptians, and Arabians, who today are all Arab and all Muslim. Roman legions in the east part of the empire started taking recruits from the people in the province in which they were based. The Tenth Legion, one of the four legions that destroyed the Temple, was based in Syria for seventy years before AD 70. The book *Daniel Revisited* shows the evidence for all of these conclusions."

"Sounds good. Let's move on," said Joe.

"So going back to Daniel 8, the five parts of the vision likely show us a chain of events in which the fifth and last part is in the Tribulation. But it all starts with the first and second part—the ram in verses 3 and 4. Look at the ram in the very first verse of the vision in verse 3. Go ahead and read it from your New King James."

The pastor read, "Then I lifted my eyes and saw, and there, standing beside the river, was a ram which had two horns, and the two horns were high; but one was higher than the other, and the higher one came up last."

Mike said, "My NIV says something similar, but with a couple of differences. First, the NIV says the horns are long instead of high. Second, and more significant, where the NKJV says the second horn comes up last, the NIV says the second horn 'grew up later.' This shows that some time goes by between the appearances of the two ram's horns. So, the second horn came up last and came up later, after the establishment of the first horn. Now, you probably know what horns typically represent in prophetic visions."

"Power, I believe," responded the pastor.

"That's right. And the power represented by a horn can be wielded by a single person like a king, or a group of people, or a whole nation and still represent power. The ram has two horns—two power bases—when the ram runs out in verse 4 during the invasion.

"And, as it so happens, in Iran one power base, or horn, was established at the beginning, and the other has grown up over the last four decades. So now the second power base has grown up to be equal to or greater than the first!"

"That's remarkable," Joe said. "But, Mike, you said 'the beginning'—the beginning of what?"

"By 'beginning' I mean the founding of the Islamic Republic of Iran, back in 1979."

THREE

IRAN THE INVADER

"**B**ut before we can talk about the horns and what they represent," Mike said, "we need to look at what the ram represents. Identifying the right country as the invader reveals the powers the two horns represent. It also shows how the geopolitics of the Middle East today are geared now toward fulfillment of Daniel 8."

"But in the popular prophecy view," Joe broke in, "the ram is ancient Persia and it runs out in three directions."

"That's right. But if this vision is to be fulfilled in the end times, we need to identify the nation or nations that would be the ram. There is an interpretation of the vision given later in Daniel 8 to help us. In Daniel 8:20 in my NIV it says, 'The two-horned ram that you saw represents the kings of Media and Persia.'"

As Mike unfolded a map on the table, he said, "This might help clarify things. You can see the modern nation of Iran with its boundaries, its capital Tehran, and its holy city of Qom just south of Tehran. Do you see the three areas with dashed lines as borders inside Iran? These are three areas that were the homelands of three ancient peoples mentioned in the Bible."

As the two men looked at the map, Mike continued. "The one furthest north is the homeland of the Medes—Media. Their ancient capital was a city called Ecbatana. You can see the modern city of Qom is in the area of ancient Media, and Tehran is just outside of the region of Media. Further south you can see the region of Elam with its old capital Susa."

Map of modern Iran and ancient homelands within Iran.

"Is that the same Susa that's mentioned in Daniel 8:2?" asked Joe, looking down at his Bible.

"Yes, it is. And we'll see more about Susa in a moment."

Mike continued, "Next, the region furthest south is Persia and its old capital at Persepolis. The peoples of the three regions each established an empire, one after the other. Each successive empire was greater and covered more area than the one before it. The Elamites established an empire first, conquering areas beyond its homeland. The Medes established the next empire which covered most of modern Iran. They conquered Persia, but not Elam. Elam was conquered and held by the Babylonians—you know, King Nebuchadnezzar.

"Anyway, the Medes' last king was actually the grandfather of the Persian king, Cyrus the Great. In building the Persian empire, Cyrus then conquered all of Iran, including Elam and Media, and dethroned his grandfather, the last Median king.

"The map shows us that the homelands of the Medes and Persians are completely inside the modern nation of Iran. Elam is included on the map to show the significance and location of Susa."

Joe leaned forward to inspect the map again.

Mike continued, "By the way, it was this sequence of kings—first the Medes and then the Persians—that fit in nicely with the way theologians were thinking in past centuries about Daniel 8. They always thought the first horn of the ram was the kings of the Medes and the second horn that grew up later and more powerful was the kings of the Persians."

Mike continued. "So we agree there is a major problem with this picture? If Daniel 8 is to be fulfilled in the end times, the horns cannot be those ancient kings. Daniel 8:4 clearly says the ram runs out with two horns—two powers. But, at the time Cyrus the Great, the king of the Persian Empire, ran out across the Middle East, there was only one horn in effect—one power, not two. The first horn was already removed when Cyrus dethroned the last king of Media. But as I will show you shortly, the ram will indeed be running out here in the end times with two horns and therefore two powerbases.

"Geographically, Iran includes Media and Persia. The Iranians today are descended in part from the Persians and Medes. The nation of Iran was called Persia up to 1935. At that time the Iranian people wanted the name changed because Persia was too restrictive—it referred only to the single region in southern Iran as shown on the map. Iran referred to all the regions—Persia, Media, and all the others.

"Back in 1971, the Shah of Iran had a big celebration. You probably didn't hear about it."

Joe said, "No, I didn't."

"That was when the ruler of Iran, the Shah Pahlavi, held a major celebration in Persepolis, commemorating the 2,500th anniversary of the founding of the Persian Empire.[1]

"So, from all this we know the country represented by the ram is modern-day Iran. The people of Iran are descended from the Medes and Persians, and the government of Iran itself at one time celebrated its ancient Persian heritage. There can be little doubt that the modern version of the Medes and Persians is anything but Iran.

"Now, Daniel 8:20 says the ram with the two horns is the kings of Media and Persia. So, those two horns are the powers in Iran, and the kings or leaders of Iran would possess that power, if the fulfillment is here in the end times."

"Agreed," Joe responded.

Mike continued, "The equivalent of a king today would be an absolute ruler such as a dictator, whether religious or militaristic. I will show you the first horn of the ram is fulfilled by the supreme leader of Iran, and the second horn is fulfilled by the IRGC."

"The IR . . . what?"

"Oh, sorry. The Iranian Revolutionary Guard Corps—the IRGC. Some call it the *Islamic* Revolutionary Guard Corps. Anyway, when the Islamic Republic of Iran was founded in 1979, a constitution was written, and Ayatollah Khomeini was made absolute ruler—the supreme leader of Iran. The constitution of Iran also created the IRGC as a special religious army to protect the supreme leader and the new Iranian Revolution. So just like the ram has two horns, Iran today has two power bases—the supreme leader, and the IRGC—that together control all political and military power in Iran."

"So, you're saying the regime in present-day Iran was foretold in Daniel 8?"

"Yes, and this interpretation of Daniel foretells more than that; it also speaks to the regime's history."

FOUR

FIRST STEP FULFILLED

The two men finished their hot drinks before getting back into the discussion. Mike Branch was sensing the same urgency he always felt as he shared this message with others. But he knew he needed to go step by step to make it perfectly clear. From the look on Joe's face, he clearly had questions.

"Mike, you said earlier you believe the fulfillment of the vision of the ram and goat has already started? What makes you think that?"

"Well, in the beginning of the vision in Daniel 8:3, it mentions the second horn grew up—that has already likely been fulfilled by the IRGC. And this is the reason I believe the invasion is next: Daniel 8:4 tells of the invasion itself right after the second horn grew up. If Daniel 8:3 has been fulfilled, time is running out until the invasion."

When Mike said "time is running out," Pastor Joe leaned forward, his eyes sharply fixed on the other man and said, "Even if the vision of the ram and goat applies to today, it's strange to think of the vision as already starting to be fulfilled. There's no invasion yet! In my mind, the growth of the second horn pales in comparison to the ram's actual charge."

"I agree," responded Mike. "But, here's the thing. We are in the end times, and we need to pay attention to every last verse and phrase to understand what's happening."

"Yes, I can see that. Just the way you showed me with verses 17 and 19," the pastor said nodding.

"The vision of the ram and goat indeed begins with the second horn growing taller and longer than the first horn, and doing it after the first horn comes up. So, Daniel 8:3 is the opening act—part 1 as we saw on the chart. The one horn takes time to grow longer and higher than the other. When the ram finally does run out, as we see in Daniel 8:4, both horns are fully grown.

"From recent history in Iran, it looks like the growing time has already passed. So now we are waiting for the invasion itself to start."

"So, how was Daniel 8:3 actually fulfilled?" asked Joe.

"Well, let's start with the text of Daniel 8:3 itself. It says in my NIV, 'I looked up, and there before me was a ram with two horns, standing beside the canal, and the horns were long. One of the horns was longer than the other but grew up later.' In the vision, the ram has two horns. And we agree horns represent power."

"Right."

"And so a horn can either be wielded by one person like a king, or a horn could be wielded by an army or even a country. The horns are long, which means the power of the two horns is great or very dominating. There are eight horns altogether in this vision. Daniel 8 tells us which horns stand for people and which stand for whole countries. Daniel 8:20 says the ram's two horns are kings—people."

Joe asked, "You mentioned the supreme leader . . . could one horn of the ram be the supreme leader of Iran?"

"That's right. When the Islamic Republic of Iran was founded, a constitution was written. The constitution of Iran says the supreme leader should be the most learned cleric in Iran. He actually speaks for their god—Allah. Whatever the supreme leader says is to be carried out. He is the one who holds real power in Iran. Candidates for the elections of the president of Iran and the parliament are all vetted by the supreme leader and the Assembly of Experts. The Assembly also has the power to elect a new supreme leader when the old one dies. In 1979 when the Islamic Republic was founded, you remember, the Ayatollah Khomeini was made the first supreme leader."

"Yes, I do," said Joe. "Khomeini was a memorable leader. OK, so that's one horn on the ram, with the power of that horn wielded by the supreme leader. You say the other is the IRGC? So then, is it the power that grew up later and is longer?"

"Yes. What has been going on in Iran since 1979 really is incredible as far as the fulfillment of Daniel 8:3 goes."

"I'd be interested in hearing more about that," said the pastor.

"Well, in 1979, the Islamic Republic of Iran was founded and the supreme leader had all the power. At the same time, the constitution also set up a bodyguard for the supreme leader, the IRGC. Just like Caesar's Praetorian Guard, it started only as a bodyguard. The constitution says that the purpose of the IRGC is to protect the supreme leader and Iran's Islamic Revolution, which we can talk about later. Both jobs are really one and the same because the supreme leader is looked upon as the leader of their Revolution.

"But, what changed the status of the IRGC was the Iran-Iraq War, which started in 1980 when Saddam Hussein invaded Iran's southwestern province, and went on for eight years."

"Yes, I remember that," said Joe. "It went on for a long time."

"Yes, the Iran-Iraq War raged through most of the 1980s. During those years Ayatollah Khomeini, the supreme leader, called millions of young people to martyrdom. Iran's regular military defended Iranian territory, but the IRGC was used for the offensive. The IRGC grew in size and power enough to take over the military during those years. So, when Saddam Hussein invaded, defending the Revolution grew in scope to defending Iran itself. To help with the defense, a volunteer corps called the Basij was started. The word *Basij* literally means 'mobilization.' Remember those Iranian teens called by the hundreds of thousands to run across minefields and throw themselves at Iraqi army positions?"

"Yes, I think I do," responded the pastor.

"They were the Basij. Today the Basij has perhaps a million or more volunteers. They are also the morality police in Iran. They provide the pool of manpower from which the IRGC takes recruits."

"Imagine a million volunteer zealots," said Joe, shaking his head.

"When the war ended in 1988, all those IRGC and Basij soldiers needed jobs and housing. They were in their teens and twenties before the war, living with their parents, but as grownups they needed housing of their own. The IRGC started a major civilian construction company to build houses for its troops. Houses and jobs were provided. The profits were used to buy up or start more businesses. During the 1990s the IRGC came to own more and more of the Iranian economy.[1] Today, the IRGC speculates in real estate abroad.[2] It took over hi-tech businesses including Iran's telecommunications company.[3] It also took over a large slice of the oil industry.[4]"

"What about the economic sanctions placed on Iran?" Joe interjected, "Didn't that hurt the IRGC?"

"No. It actually had the opposite effect. Foreign companies that were bidding on construction or oil projects were forced to leave Iran and not do business there. The projects were still needed, so the IRGC filled in the void, running with next to no competition.[5] Today it is said the IRGC directly controls companies making up around 40 percent of the Iranian economy.[6] The profits derived from all of these industries are used in part by the IRGC to acquire weapon systems, pay IRGC salaries, bribe politicians, fund terror groups, and recruit new members using financial incentives such as cheap housing.

"From the mid-1990s to the mid-2000s, the IRGC became involved with both state security and national politics. IRGC Intelligence and the Basij replaced the older security and intelligence ministries. The IRGC's involvement with politics was due to its growing power. The IRGC's support of Mahmoud Ahmadinejad, a former Basij commander, for his first term as president in 2005, was evidence of the IRGC's involvement in national politics. Remember him?"

"He would be a hard man to forget," said Joe. "He seemed like an extremist even compared to the Ayatollahs. What happened to him?"

Mike smiled and answered, "They're actually *all* extremists—Ahmadinejad is just very outspoken. Anyway, he left the presidency of Iran when his two terms were up, in accordance with their constitution. With its growing influence through the years, the IRGC made Ahmadinejad president for a second term. They had witnessed his statements and actions, and had seen who he was. He 'won' the election in 2009, against all popular opposition," said Mike, gesturing quote marks with his fingers.

"Didn't he actually win?" asked Joe.

"Well, the Basij stuffed ballot boxes in some of the provinces, allowing Ahmadinejad to win a second term.[7] At that point it could be said that the IRGC had the power to control who could be president. Though the supreme leader chooses the candidates who will run for president in Iran, the IRGC can greatly affect who will be president. The election of Mahmoud Ahmadinejad as Iran's sixth president greatly benefitted the IRGC. Ahmadinejad awarded a record two-thirds of the cabinet positions to former IRGC commanders. This allowed the IRGC to continue to expand in domestic influence, and, in particular, banking, and the oil industry."

Mike Branch continued. "The IRGC's power has increased to the point that experts now wonder who is truly more powerful— the supreme leader or the IRGC.[8] It has also gotten to the point now where both powers actually need each other."

"Need each other? How's that?"

"Well, the supreme leader needs the IRGC's military might to stay in power. It's estimated that perhaps three quarters or more of the Iranian people hate the current regime and want to see it end."

"That's amazing that three quarters of the people hate the regime," said Joe.

"Sure is. So, you can see how the supreme leader actually needs the IRGC to keep his position. The IRGC on the other hand is led by men who have a religious ideology. They would never take over even though they probably could, because a cult of the supreme leader is at the center of their ideology. In other words, the supreme leader gives them legitimacy—a reason for them to exist as the IRGC."

"Is the IRGC more powerful than the supreme leader now?" asked Joe.

"We cannot know exactly if the second horn has grown longer and become more powerful than the first horn, so right now, I'd say it's a tossup. This process of growth of the IRGC has gone on for all the years since 1979. Experts on Iran tell us the supreme leader still exercises the real power in Iran. What the elected president or parliament says is kept in line by the supreme leader. The IRGC backs the supreme leader, supports him, and can exercise military influence both inside and outside Iran. The IRGC's power also comes from running the rocket forces, the nuclear program, perhaps half of the Iranian economy, and controlling the Basij. Another arm of the IRGC called the Quds Force is already in Iraq, Lebanon, Syria and Yemen helping terrorist groups and assisting Assad in Syria."

Mike paused a moment before saying, "The moment when the second horn is actually longer than the first horn may have already happened. That is why I think we are living on borrowed time."

The words "borrowed time" seemed to greatly interest Joe Taylor.

"Yes, the invasion could happen anytime."

"Anytime?" echoed Joe.

"Yes, and that's why it's so urgent to get the word out. We can be reasonably sure the invasion is next. Remember, in Daniel 8, the invasion is the very next event after the second horn grows longer. So, you see, there is a compelling case that the power of the IRGC, which grew up later and became more powerful after the supreme leader received his power, is a very possible fulfillment of Daniel 8:3."

Mike continued, "There is another factor, too, associated with the IRGC being the fulfillment of Daniel 8:20 as well. That's where it talks about the two horns being the 'kings.' The leaders of the IRGC today include a handful of men who all entered the IRGC at the same time back in 1980 when the Iran-Iraq War first broke out. They all fought in the war, rose through the ranks and made the IRGC not only a lifetime career but also their religion, so to speak. One man controls the Quds Force and its financing and international military moves. One is the chief of staff for all the Iranian military. Another is the commander of the IRGC. Yet another is the head of IRGC headquarters and controls the money and the supplying of the IRGC. These men—along with the supreme leader—may be the kings."

"But, wouldn't there be two kings, just like the two horns?" asked Joe.

"Just because there are two horns and Daniel 8:20 says they are the kings, doesn't mean there have to be literally two men. The first horn is likely the one man—the supreme leader. But the second horn could represent several 'kings.' The two horns represent power, not a count of personnel. If this is the proper interpretation, then the generals of the IRGC could indeed be the kings. All have risen personally in their careers from infantrymen in the field, through the ranks gaining more power, until they took over the IRGC they joined."

"I can see that," said Joe. "Let me see if I've got this straight about the ram and horns. The ram is Iran. Two powers govern Iran—one is theocratic and wielded by the supreme leader."

"Right," Mike said, "and the second is militaristic and has sworn an oath to the supreme leader. This second horn is wielded by a handful of men who form a group who are all about the same age having fought together, ruled together, mourned losses of brothers and comrades together, over four decades. These may very well be the kings of Media and Persia of Daniel 8:20."

"OK, what's next?"

"The invasion is next. The ram will 'run out,' just like Daniel says."

FIVE

THE INVASION: NORTH, WEST, AND SOUTH

"This is getting really interesting," Pastor Joe said, looking down at his Bible open to Daniel 8. "Daniel 8:20 told us what the ram is, and Daniel 8:3 told us that one power grows up later after the first power. So, what's left is Daniel 8:4."

"That's right," Mike said. "In that verse, we see the invasion itself—we see what Iran will do. Daniel 8:4 says in my NIV, 'I watched the ram as he charged toward the west and the north and the south. No animal could stand against him, and none could rescue from his power. He did as he pleased and became great.'

"Let's take this verse in two pieces. The first part is the actual invasion and the second part is the idea that Iran will get to do all it wants to do. So, if the interpretation we've talked about so far is correct, it looks like Iranian military forces, likely the IRGC including the Basij, will run out in three directions."

"Run out from where and to where?" The pastor asked.

"It looks like, from Daniel 8:2, that the starting place is Susa. My NIV reads, 'In my vision I saw myself in the citadel of Susa in the province of Elam.' Remember that was the old capital of Elam we talked about."

"Ah, yes."

"If we take what Daniel 8:2–4 says literally, Iranian forces will run out from Susa. Daniel saw the ram standing by the canal, or river, while he was at Susa. So, in Daniel's view, it charged out from Susa."

"Does it have to be Susa? I mean, maybe it can be from anywhere and Susa is just where Daniel happened to be," suggested Joe.

"Well, you're right," said Mike, "It could be from anywhere in Iran. But there seems to be an excellent military strategic reason why the invasion should actually start at Susa. Look at this other map of the Middle East."

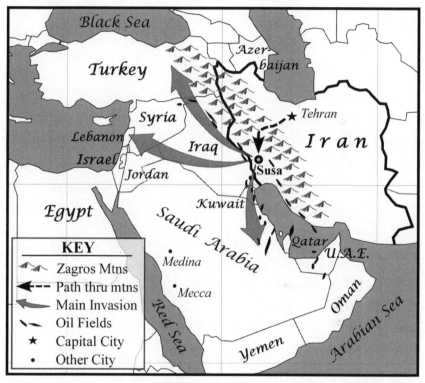

Map of the Middle East showing Iran, with the starting area around Susa, and the three directions in which the invasion would progress.

The two men looked down at the map Mike had unfolded. "You see, most of Iran is east of the Zagros Mountains, which you can see run north to south. The range does a fairly good job of cutting off Iran from the rest of the Middle East. And you can see in the western part of Iran, following its western border with Iraq, there are the Zagros Mountains. Those mountains aren't terribly high, but they are rugged; transportation corridors through the mountains are few.

Most of the Iranian forces would have to cross this mountain range. This would mean tanks, vehicles and other mobile forces would have to go single file."

"But, that would hamper an invasion," said Joe. "If you were an invading general, I would think you'd want all your forces ready to move forward."

"Yes," said Mike, his finger on the map. "But, as the map shows us, there is one place—and only one place in all of Iran—from which forces could be amassed to stage an attack on the Middle East to the west and south. That's on the plain in the southwest corner of Iran."

"What's there?"

"It's the Iranian province of Khuzestan."

"And where is Susa?"

"Right there, in Khuzestan. To carry out an invasion you would likely want all your forces to move out at the same time. If you invade from *east* of the Zagros Mountains, your forces would have to go out single file on the road over the mountains. But, if you gather them *west* of the mountains, in the plain around Susa, you could send them all out unhindered at the same time to the north, south and west. The terrain is fairly flat; there are several highways in the three directions . . . and the starting area is populated by friendly Shia Muslims."

"That all makes sense," said Joe. "In fact, it's remarkable! The geography of Iran would only allow an invasion from the place where Daniel was seeing the vision."

"Yes, it all fits together."

"But, where would the three directions go exactly? And what would be in those three directions?"

"Well, let's look at each one," responded Mike. "Let's start with the west. The word used in the Hebrew for 'west' in Daniel 8:4 is *yawm* which means 'sea' or 'seacoast.' Looking at the map, you can see that Iran's forces running west from Susa could reach the Mediterranean coast. They would completely occupy Iraq, Syria, and Lebanon, and perhaps a part of Jordan."

"Would Israel be invaded or attacked?" asked Pastor Joe, looking concerned.

"It might be attacked. But we know, according to Daniel 9:27, Israel is intact later at the start of the Tribulation. Other end-time prophecies talk about the Antichrist's forces invading Israel. So we know Israel is still there after the Iranian invasion. I want to talk about that in a moment, but the Iranian regime has a specific agenda, and Israel is actually not at the top of their list. Besides, look at the map. Iranian forces would have to first invade and occupy a host of Arab countries. To successfully attack Israel's military, Iran would have to use a concentration of most of its forces. As it turns out, this Iranian invasion of the Middle East is actually going to start a great Sunni-Shia War, fought only between Muslims."

"Ah, yes, the Sunni and Shia," said Joe, "the two major factions of Islam."

"That's right, pastor. And they've been at odds with each other for the whole history of Islam since Muhammad died—fourteen centuries ago. Again, Iran's invasion would be the start of a great Sunni-Shia War. Most of the territory Iran's forces would run out across in those three directions would be over Sunni territory."

Joe looked thoughtful as he traced a route on the map. "So perhaps Iran's forces would reach the Mediterranean Sea up in Lebanon or Syria and perhaps down south of Israel towards the Red Sea?"

"Yes. And the nations that would be caught in this westward push by Iran would be Iraq, Syria and Lebanon—which are already controlled or heavily influenced by Iran. Jordan might be affected too. I drew the arrows on the map to show those four nations being involved."

"What would Iran want to do there? There is no particular target, it seems." Joe shook his head.

"Well, Iran's overarching strategy is to spread their brand of Islamic Revolution. The Iranian regime believes their Revolution is a blueprint to building a better Islamic society—a Shia society. Everywhere they go they might try to instill this new way to rule. Let's look at that after we see the three directions."

"OK. Oh, but what about ISIS? That's to the west also, right?"

"Yes. If ISIS is still there in Syria or northern Iraq when Iran runs out, Iran would quickly destroy it."

"Do you mean Iran could have always destroyed ISIS?"

"Likely, yes. I think Iran has been holding back and using ISIS as an excuse to invade to the west. The IRGC has also used the ISIS battlefield as a way to improve its own tactics and internal military organization.[1] Iran will then control not only the Shia areas of Iraq and Syria, as it does today, but will occupy and rule the Sunni areas as well. That's all of Iraq and Syria and likely Lebanon as well."

"Ok. What's next—the north?" asked Joe as he glanced down at the map.

"Right. To the north, you can see on the map the only areas are northern Iraq and eastern Turkey. There isn't much out that way, except some of Iraq's oil fields in the northern part of that country. There are some Shia Muslims in eastern Turkey, as well as the Kurds. Iran might try to instill some new Shiite or Kurdish state in eastern Turkey, but this is just speculation. Occupying eastern Turkey also might just be a ploy to tie down Turkey's rather large forces. That way they'd be occupied so they couldn't fight elsewhere in the Middle East, at least not at first. Turkey's military is the only one large enough among the Muslim states to present a threat to the IRGC."

"Is there any other place they might invade up north?"

"Well, there is Azerbaijan. Occupying Azerbaijan is another possibility."

"Tell me about Azerbaijan," said Joe. "I'm not too familiar with that country."

"It's a smaller nation, bordering Iran in its northwest area, as you can see on the map. Before the Soviet Union came along it used to be part of Iranian territory. The people are related to the Iranians and they are Shia Muslims. Iran might decide with the ensuing chaos of war to take it back. This is just speculation."

"Very interesting."

"But don't forget," said Mike, "in all this speculation as to where the IRGC might go, what's important is what the Bible seems to be telling us. It tells us Iranian forces will run out in three directions from Susa and be successful. That's about all we can really know at this point."

"Granted; a good thing to remember," answered the pastor.

"Look at what's to the south," Mike said. "Of the three directions, I think the worst impact to Muslims and to the world in general will be to the south of Susa."

"Let me look at the map again. There are quite a few nations to the south, aren't there?"

"Yes, this is where things get really interesting. Iran will likely occupy several nations as you can see from the southern arrow on the map. The nations would include Saudi Arabia, Kuwait, Qatar, and the United Arab Emirates—the UAE—as well as tiny Bahrain not shown on the map, and possibly Oman. Much of the world's oil is there—the Gulf oil fields—the oil of Saudi Arabia and all the Gulf countries. With its own oil, the Gulf oil, and the oil in northern Iraq, Iran would control one quarter of the world's daily oil production."

"Wow!" the pastor responded. "I knew the Middle East had a lot of oil but I didn't realize it was that much. But, I guess that makes sense. Otherwise, why would much of the world worry about what happens in the Middle East?"

Mike nodded. "It's always been interesting to me that God is working his plans in the Middle East in the end times. America, China, and the nations of Europe have great economic and military influence in the world, but God has arranged for one-fourth of the world's economic lifeblood to be buried underneath the desert waste that is the Middle East. During this great invasion, Iran would use that fact to its advantage. Remember the oil embargo of the 70s?"

"Sure. I remember sitting with my dad in his car in line for gas; it seemed like we waited forever."

"Back in 1973, and again in 1979, about 6 percent of the world's oil production got cut off. It caused oil prices to triple in 1973 and then to double again in 1979. The price didn't go down either between 1973 and 1979. It caused Americans like you and your dad to sit in lines that were blocks long, waiting for their turn at the pump."

"Yeah, I remember seeing it on the news when I was a kid, too."

"Me too," said Mike. "Well, this wouldn't be a 6 percent cut. It'd be a 25 percent cut. A one-quarter cut in oil, possibly. If Iran wanted to cut off the oil from any particular area, or all areas, it could. Remember the words of Daniel 8:4: 'No animal could stand against him, and none could rescue from his power. He did as he pleased and became great.'"

"I doubt that could *really* happen." Joe sounded a bit skeptical. "The United States would never allow it."

"I've heard many people say that. But God's Word says what it says. If this interpretation is true, it will happen. The United States of the past—under Reagan or Bush—might not have allowed Iran to invade the Middle East. But the United States of other presidents might let it go. For instance, we've watched the Obama administration for years encouraging Iran to expand militarily. The nuclear deal is an example."

"Yes," I've been following that, said Joe. "I believe the details of that deal actually do nothing to stop Iran from building an atomic bomb."

"So whether our military is crippled somehow, or our economy collapses, or there is an EMP—you know, an electro-magnetic pulse attack, or the administration just doesn't want to stop Iran . . . whatever the reason, the Bible tells us *no one*—and that includes the United States—will stop Iran."

Pastor Joe's shoulders sagged as he contemplated the consequences of an attack.

"In addition," said Mike, "what if another president comes along who actually orders a major attack on Iran? What if he sent in an army as large as or larger than the one used to oust Saddam Hussein in 2003? Even that attack would be defeated if we are reading God's Word correctly."

"I'd hate to think of that happening to our nation," said Joe.

"Me too." Mike continued, "There are other physical and military factors, too, that might be part of the equation to allow Iran to do all it wants. Iran might have nuclear bombs at that point. No country interferes too much with a nuclear power. Also, Russia sold the S-300 missile anti-aircraft system to Iran. It's basically impenetrable for any air force except by the US Air Force using several of its best stealth aircraft.²"

"The nuclear factor would definitely weigh in," said Joe.

"And there's something else beyond the possible loss of oil. There's the whole matter of the US petrodollar to consider."

"The petrodollar?" asked the pastor. "I've heard of it but I'm not sure what that is."

"The petrodollar is a financial system set up in the '70s by Henry Kissinger. The US dollar was supported by the gold standard until 1971. After that, the dollar needed support from another source. So, the Nixon administration set up a deal with the Saudi monarchy: in exchange for guaranteed military protection from outside invasion, Saudi Arabia and the oil sheikdoms of the Gulf would sell all their oil only in US dollars. This is one reason there are large US air bases in those countries—so the US can defend them."

"That's really interesting," said Joe. "I sure haven't read much about that."

"Since many developed nations in Asia and Europe were buying oil from the Middle East, those nations had to continue to keep their foreign currency reserves in US dollars. Nations had held on to US dollars beforehand simply because they were stable due to being on the gold standard. But with the gold standard gone, the dollar was losing its value. With the petrodollar system, the US dollar was stabilized again, being priced in terms of barrels of oil, because other nations had to have more dollars to purchase oil. Remember Operation Desert Storm?" asked Mike.

"Sure do."

"We went into Kuwait and liberated it from Saddam Hussein's invasion in 1991. That was our honoring of the petrodollar agreement as Kuwait sold its oil only in dollars. Now the Iranian regime has already stated its goal of diminishing the use of the US dollar."

"That doesn't sound as if it would be very good for us," said Joe, frowning.

"Right. What Iran could do to the US petrodollar might be as bad as or even worse economically than the hit on the oil supply. When Iran takes all the oil fields in the Middle East it could easily cut off the oil. Or it could continue to sell it but demand another currency or gold as payment. Very high oil prices coupled with the devaluing of the US dollar would have great ramifications for the US and world economy. We'll revisit this a little later, but before we do, we need to finish looking at Daniel 8:4. The second part of the verse shows us that Iran will not be stopped."

SIX

DESIRE OF THE REGIME

"Read it out loud again from your NKJV version, Joe."

Joe read, "I saw the ram pushing westward, northward, and southward, so that no animal could withstand him; nor *was there any* that could deliver from his hand, but he did according to his will and became great."

When Joe finished reading, Mike said, "We talked about the first part of this verse—how the ram ran out in three directions. And we talked about how no nation would be able to stop the Iranian forces, not even America. So now let's look at the next, and last, part of the verse where it says 'but he did according to his will and became great.'"

"That sounds like the invasion could be ominous," Joe said. "I've seen news stories over the years about what is important to the leaders of Iran. Some of them mentioned 'wiping' Israel off the map. They're calling the US the Great Satan, and chanting death threats."

"Yes, the western media only touched on a few of the things they thought might be sensational. The Iranian leadership has more items on its shopping list of things it would want to do during its invasion."

"Like what?" asked Joe, his brow furrowed.

"There are basically three things the Iranian regime wants to do. First, as we talked about earlier, they want to export the brand of Islamic revolution they had in 1979 in Iran to every Muslim country."

"Hmm. That would be a mess."

"For sure. Second, they want to cause chaos throughout all Islamic countries."

"What on earth for?"

"They believe this will hasten the return of their messiah, someone they call *al-Mahdi*."

"That's a name I've never heard," said Joe.

"And third, they want to hurt the western powers, most notably the United States—the 'Great Satan.' All three of these goals can be achieved by their invasion."

"What about Israel?" inquired the pastor. "Haven't they said they want to wipe Israel off the map?"

"Well, not quite," answered Mike.

"Not quite? What do you mean?"

"The western media has said Iran wants to wipe Israel off the map. Some sources have said that was a mistranslation. What the regime really said is they want to remove the name of Israel from the pages of history. They have also called that an *ultimate goal*. But, the Iranian regime has more immediate goals which I'll explain. This gets a little complicated, but hang in there with me. Everything the Iranian regime wants to do is based on its brand of Islamic belief. It's called *Twelver Shia*."

Joe said, "Well, of course I've heard of Shia—that's the minority denomination of Islam. Sunni makes up the majority, right?"

"Right. And within Shia Islam, like any religious denomination, there are varying shades of beliefs. Iran is peopled mostly by Shia Muslims, and about 85 percent of the Shia population of Iran is Twelver Shia. Now, a Shia Muslim in general believes their founding prophet Muhammad designated a specific successor to be the leader of Islam, also called the caliph, and the Twelver Shia believes there will be exactly twelve successors.

"Just for comparison with Shia Muslims, Sunni Muslims believe the successors started with a man named Abu Bakr, who became caliph on Muhammad's death. The line of successors continued on down to the twentieth century. These were the caliphs ruling in the office known as the caliphate. By the way, the Turks ended the office in 1924."

Mike went on. "Anyway, the Twelver Shias believe they have seen eleven successors and they are now waiting for the twelfth. The twelfth and last successor, or imam, as Shia Muslims call them, is called al-Mahdi, or simply Mahdi. According to Islamic writings, he will unite and rule Islam for seven years. The way this man is described is similar to the Bible's description of the Antichrist, ruling for seven years during the Tribulation. Anyway, the Twelfth Imam is said to have disappeared in the tenth century AD and is to reappear toward the end of the age and will rule Islam. The Mahdi is also called the 'Hidden Imam.' The world is now in a period they call the 'Occultation of the Imam.' The fact that many Iranians are Twelver Shias means that many Iranians are waiting for the Mahdi to appear. This is a major motivation for what Iran will do to fulfill the passages about the ram in Daniel 8.

"The founder of the Iranian Revolution, Ayatollah Ruhollah Khomeini, was a Twelver.[1] His successor, current supreme leader Ayatollah Ali Khamenei is also a Twelver, and so is the leadership of the IRGC. In the years prior to 1979, back when the Shah still ruled Iran, the man who was going to be the first supreme leader, Ayatollah Khomeini, was formulating his ideas of how to run an Islamic society. He wrote a book titled *Velayat-e Faqih*, which in English is the *Guardianship of the Jurisprudent*."

"What was that all about?" Joe asked, looking puzzled.

"Khomeini believed there needed to be a better system of ruling an Islamic society while in the Occultation of the Imam—the time of waiting for the Twelfth Imam to appear. The rule of sharia law over society, or the *Jurisprudent*, needs to be guarded by the wisest leader. And so, this supposed leader, called the Islamic jurist, or guardian, needs to be the most informed and educated among all Islamic clerics. Hence the name of the book, the *Guardianship of the Jurisprudent*."

"I agree. This is a little complicated. Interesting, though," said Joe.

"Well, I warned you," Mike chuckled. "Back in 1979, Iranians recognized Ayatollah Khomeini as that man. As it is with most revolutions, Iranians thought Khomeini would liberate their country from the oppression of the Shah. When the Shah was finally ousted, Khomeini took over as that one leader, making his ideology of the one guardian ruling an Islamic society a reality. The problem, of course, was that Iranians traded one form of oppression for another that was worse. Khomeini's position as supreme leader was written as the foundation of the current Iranian constitution. This highest ruler is called the *Faqih*, or the Guardian, who shepherds the Muslim flock until Mahdi appears. Establishing this guardianship over society is what the Iranian regime calls their Revolution. It's sort of their version of what we Americans call our American Revolution—a major change in the way our society is run. The Iranians also refer to the 1979 revolution as the *Revolution*, with a capital R.

"What makes the Iranian regime especially dangerous with their Revolution, is that their ideology also says their Revolution needs to exist in *all* Muslim countries, not just Iran. They believe all of Islam should be ruled their way until al-Mahdi appears.[2] And being the only major Shia nation, they would spread their Shia Revolution to mostly Sunni nations."

"I can't see the Sunni nations going along with this without a fight," said Joe, shaking his head.

"Yes, it would be a great provocation for a large, intense religious war. Khomeini founded the Quds Force within the IRGC in 1981. The sole purpose of the Quds Force is to export their Revolution to other Muslim countries. Today, the Quds Force, under General Soleimani, is doing just that. They're working with terrorists and Shia militants in various countries around the Middle East to effect change in governments in those countries. Khomeini's desire to export the Revolution was also a reason why the Iran-Iraq War dragged on for eight years. After the Iranians expelled Saddam Hussein and the Iraqi forces from Iran in 1982, the war could have ended at that time. But the war continued for six more years, with Khomeini trying to force the Revolution on Iraq, and Saddam trying to contain Iran."

"That helps me better understand Iran's motivation," said Joe.

"Good," said Mike. "Remember, as we talked about earlier, Saddam's initial invasion is what triggered the growth of the IRGC, the second horn of the ram."

"The IRGC leadership is charged with defending the Revolution, and spreading it. Spreading the Revolution is also very much a part of the IRGC leadership's ideology. Do you remember hearing any of the speeches of Mahmoud Ahmadinejad, the last president of Iran?"

"Sure," answered Joe. "He was the one who the world thought was a nut."

"Well, everyone might have thought he was a religious nut, but he believed the same things that the supreme leader and IRGC believe— he was just outspoken about it. At one point, he said the Revolution in Iran is not just about changing the government of Iran, but the Revolution wants to be a world government.[3]

"He was also a big believer in the coming of Mahdi. Ahmadinejad began each of his major campaign speeches with a prayer for the early return of the Mahdi.[4] As president of Iran, he spoke at the United Nations each year about the coming of Mahdi.[5] I read his speeches— they're available on the Internet.[6] He talked openly of everyone needing to take part in bringing about the coming of al-Mahdi."

"I wonder how many in the West were paying attention," said Joe. "I wasn't."

"The world ignored the rants of someone they viewed as a nut. And he said all these things prior to his campaign to run for his second term in 2009. The IRGC and Basij obviously didn't have a problem with Ahmadinejad's beliefs because they stuffed ballot boxes in several provinces in order to have him reelected. Anyway, he served his two terms per their constitution and stepped down in 2013."

"So, how do the IRGC's beliefs fit with what the Bible says?" asked Joe, his finger on Daniel 8:4.

"Like a hand in a glove!" said Mike. "The Iranian regime and its beliefs, fits perfectly with how Daniel 8:4 says the ram will run out in three directions, out over many countries. The ram will charge and butt and surprise many people. The regime will do this because they want to spread their Islamic Revolution to many countries and cause chaos to possibly speed up their Mahdi's coming. And the IRGC will have the military ability to carry it out."

"Hmm," said Joe.

"But the IRGC will do this because their ideology is basically the same as the supreme leader's. The IRGC is more than just a military, it's like a cult. Early on, following the Revolution in 1979, IRGC officers were made responsible for IRGC troop indoctrination. In essence, the IRGC was allowed to provide philosophical guidance for itself.[7] The IRGC has been able to keep its ranks ideologically pure and uniform, and to expel those who think differently. Indoctrination of guardsmen and officers is carried out at various Iranian universities."

"Do you know what the IRGC teaches?" the pastor asked.

"Yes. Unlike most Shia Muslims who are allowed to choose their own ayatollah to learn from, all IRGC members follow a cult of the supreme leader only. Their cult may be more of a following of the late Khomeini himself and his teachings, rather than of the supreme leader's office. But the leaders of the IRGC have sworn their allegiance to protect the supreme leader, uphold the office, and spread their Revolution."

Mike looked across the table at Joe and said, "I believe God has prepared the Iranian nation and its current regime to be the ram of Daniel 8. The ram will want to charge, and charge hard, all over the Middle East which is indeed to the north, west, and south of Susa. The regime wants to cause chaos in as many Muslim countries as it can—both to change the way each country is ruled and to supposedly force the coming of al-Mahdi. Ironically, if al-Mahdi is the Antichrist, then Iran is indeed going to accomplish everything it wants to accomplish, and that means *everything*."

"What does that *everything* mean to me ... and us here at home?" asked Joe.

"Well, by occupying and controlling the oil fields, it will also cause economic chaos across the world, and bring down the currency and economy of the United States. And in the end, they will indeed cause their al-Mahdi—our Antichrist—to appear."

"God help us." Joe shook his head, a look of deep concern on his face.

"Amen."

SEVEN

IMPACT ON THE WORLD

The two men had talked for some time. The last light of dusk had faded from the windows and it was now dark outside.

"I can see why our friend Richard wanted me to hear this message," Joe said. "I can think of a lot of bad things that might happen to all of us as a consequence of Iran being the ram in Daniel 8."

"Keep in mind, too," added Mike, "if these events play out we, as the church, can no longer sit back and just watch and see who is right."

"Yes, I see that. It's no longer a theoretical matter. If this is right it will bring real consequences."

Mike looked at Joe across the table and said, "What I'm about to say next is probably the most important part of the message." He hesitated for a moment. "There is going to be a tremendous impact on the world. We, as Christians, need to be ready."

"I'm ready to hear more. I can see the invasion would have serious implications."

"You remember we talked about Iran's military charging south into the Gulf oil fields, and north into northern Iraq. We also talked about how the Iranian ram will get to do all it wants to do, and that it wants to spread its Revolution wherever it can. It also wants to cause chaos so it will speed up the supposed coming of their messiah. By occupying the oil fields and controlling one-fourth of the world's oil, Iran will be set up to do all it wants to do: create chaos, spread its Revolution, and hurt the United States. Can you imagine how Iran could do this?"

"I guess one thing Iran could do is turn off the oil spigot if it wanted to, driving up the price."

"That's right. Do you realize what that would do to the global economy? Back in 1973, oil prices *tripled* when the oil supply was cut by only 6 percent. When the oil was restored the price didn't go down. And when it was cut again by only 6 percent in 1979, the price doubled. But now we are talking about a potential 25 percent cut—four times greater than what happened in 1973 or 1979. Just applying the same relative price rise corresponding to a cut four times larger, we would be looking at an oil price *twelve* times greater! In other words, if a 6 percent cut in oil causes a tripling in price, might a cut four times bigger cause a price hike twelve times over?"

"Twelve times! That sounds crazy. How would our economy withstand that?" asked Joe.

"Think about this. The world produces about ninety million barrels of oil per day, and consumes about ninety million barrels of oil per day. The USA all by itself consumes nineteen million barrels per day. What's one-fourth of ninety million—about twenty-two million? That's more oil than the USA consumes all by itself.

"The oil would be cut off to the nations that directly use the Mideast oil—countries like Japan, South Korea, Taiwan, China, as well as European countries like France and Germany. So, physically, if the oil is cut off to those countries, they would then bid on the oil available from other sources like Mexico, Venezuela, and Nigeria. That's the oil America uses. And those nations will bid up the price because they will be desperate to restore their oil supply.

"Take Japan, for instance. Fully two-thirds of Japan's energy needs are met by oil and natural gas.[1] The remaining third is nuclear, coal, and hydroelectric. Can you imagine what would happen if all its oil and gas was cut off? Japan has a sixty-day reserve, and, in that time, it would be desperately trying to buy oil from other sources. In the course of doing that, they'd bid up the price of oil to steer some oil from other sources to Japan. If Japan didn't get the oil it needs, over one hundred million Japanese might not have enough to eat, or enough fuel to stay warm. It's a nightmare scenario. Other developed countries besides Japan would also be vying for oil."

"What about the US? Aren't we now more self-sufficient in oil?" asked Joe.

"We'll still be affected. "The oil supply and price are globally interconnected. Even if the US could drill and provide all of its own oil, the price would still go up because the oil market is global. As an example, Canada overall produces more oil than it uses. You might think they would do well financially and have all the oil they need. Financially, they would indeed do fine, but most of the oil they produce is in the western part of the country and is piped or shipped to other countries like the US or China. The eastern part of Canada uses most of the oil products in that country. They need to get the oil back east to them, but right now it's going through an international supply chain. The price of their oil would go way up as well. Fortunately for Canada, they would do well financially because they would sell the oil at the same price in the west as they would buy it back in the east."

"But, couldn't we just drill for more oil?" asked Joe.

"We could, but there are some factors working against that."

"Like what?"

"First, most of the extra oil we have is in the form of shale deposits. Much of it requires fracking, so it would take years to build up the production capacity we would need. Second, America's reserves are only the tenth largest in the world. That would feed our current consumption for only ten years. Third, there's the global market thing again—the price would still be high.[2] So, for at least a few years, America would be short on oil, and the high price would continue for some time anyway.

"Oil shortages of the kind we are talking about here would likely cause a reduction of food output, raising prices for food. A lot of the world's fertilizer is oil-based. Tractors run on gasoline. Prices for manufactured goods and just about everything we use would also go up. If oil goes up twelve times in price, so does paint, and washing machines, and roof tiles, and clothing. You get the picture."

"So when you think about it," Joe cut in, "The outlook is dismal. Oil isn't just used for transportation and electricity—it's used for everything."

"You are so right. Everything is made from oil and transported by oil. How much does a new set of tires cost? Maybe $400? How about twelve times that? You can see that the cost of merely surviving will easily outstrip most people's paychecks. This assumes that people can still get to work and get a paycheck without going into debt paying for gas, and that their workplace is still heated and lighted, and the electricity is on all the time. And then you have to think about the two-thirds of Americans, and most of the rest of the world, who live paycheck to paycheck."

"Like many in our churches," said Joe.

"Yes. And that's only one of the two major problems. We talked about one of them—the cut off of oil. The second problem is going to be a much bigger problem for America than for everyone else. Remember we were talking about the US petrodollar a few minutes ago? That's the other problem. The Iranian regime has made it clear they want to take down the dollar. In order to cause economic chaos they don't even have to shut off the oil. All they would need to do is declare all the oil in the Middle East is to be sold in any currency but dollars. The only reason many countries like South Korea or Taiwan hold large reserves of dollars is to buy oil from Mideast countries. It's also the reason they accept our dollars for payment for TVs and cars—they need the dollars to buy oil. Iran could easily say oil must be bought in gold or even Chinese renminbi. South Korea and Japan would dump their dollars and buy renminbi.

"All those nations holding dollars would start selling them. They would sell US treasuries and other forms of US debt. They would trade their cash denominated in dollars for whatever Iran wanted. And remember, Daniel 8:4 says Iran gets to do all it wants to do. It might be able to do this by threatening the entire oil infrastructure with an atomic weapon via an EMP."

"I've started hearing a little about the danger of an electromagnetic pulse," said Joe.

Mike nodded. "An EMP could come from the explosion of an atomic bomb a couple hundred miles above the earth. An EMP from a single nuclear device could make all the pumping and distributing systems in the Gulf seize up. Electrical devices and circuits in machinery would be burned out."

"I can't even imagine the hardship an EMP would cause," said Joe.

"Have you ever wondered why the troops in the Gog-Magog War in Ezekiel 38:4–5 are described as equipped with horses, swords and shields?"

"Not really. But now that you mention it, why would those things be in the end times? Why not bombers, tanks, and guns?"

"Indeed, but I don't mean to get off topic here. I mention it only to show that the idea of an EMP in the Middle East might not be that crazy. Anyway, all those dollars would find their way back to America. The demand for dollars would go way down. All those dollars printed by the Federal Reserve would no longer be sent overseas but would be used right here. When the demand for anything goes down, the price of what's demanded also goes down. The Fed would be the only buyer of all that debt being sold. And then it would become obvious that the only reason the dollar is worth as much as it is, is only because the Fed says it is. The only thing buoying the value of the dollar at that point is hope—not gold and not oil—only hope, which wouldn't last long. Now all those who still have faith in the US government and the dollar would see all their wealth go down in value. All their bank accounts, stocks, bonds, and whatever is being held in dollars. Today, ten thousand dollars will buy you a nice used car. A year after Iran has destroyed the petrodollar system you might be able to get a week's groceries with that same ten thousand."

"I can't imagine that happening here," said Joe.

"I think you touched on the big reason this Iranian invasion will be so hard on Americans—we would be dealing with problems we've never had before. Consider this," said Mike, "Every paper currency in world history has gone to zero in value. Ours hasn't yet because our government has always succeeded in having something of real value prop it up, and by doing that, creating a demand for dollars. But once the petrodollar goes away, the dollar will be backed by nothing. There will be nothing from stopping hyperinflation, like what happened to Germany in the 1920s. At that point the dollar would continue to lose value and go to zero. Imagine, everyone's bank accounts, pensions, and social security payments not being able to purchase what they did before."

"And just when the price of oil goes up on its own, too," said Joe.

"Iran could either cut off the oil or destroy the petrodollar system, or even both. The whole world would be in economic shock, both from a massive oil shortage and from the devaluation of the reserve currency of most of the world."

"Mike, aren't many nations' currencies pegged to the dollar?"

"Yes, and they'd lose their foreign currency reserves. But Americans would have it worse because if the price of oil does increase so many times over, their savings and wealth in dollars will end up being worthless, so oil would cost even more. Americans would also go through a period of added turmoil, for perhaps a few months, as the nation replaces the dollar with a new currency. Add to the oil shortages and economic distress happening across the world, we'd also be witnessing a massive war going on in the Middle East with Shia Muslims massacring Sunni Muslims and vice versa."

"Wow. That's a terrible picture you're painting," Joe said. "All that just from the ram running out. But it does make sense. It's the oil. The world has become so dependent on it and now one-quarter of it could be taken away. That would set up the world for the Antichrist, wouldn't it?"

"Yes!" answered Mike. "The current Mideast geo-political and global economic picture here in the end times seems to be showing us that chaos will reign when the Persian ram of Daniel 8 runs out. The picture is clear to me, but some in the church might need more convincing of the consequences."

"I know some in my church would, for sure."

"Well, to add another voice to the argument for possible chaos, there are other prophetic passages besides Daniel 8 that may parallel the events of Daniel 8. And they definitely confirm for us that the world will be thrown into economic chaos of an intensity that will cause great stress in most people's lives."

"Which specific Bible passages are you talking about?" asked Joe.

"Well, we talked about how Daniel 8 changed our perception of the origin of the Antichrist from Europe to the Middle East. That, in turn, changes our interpretation of Daniel 2:40 and the iron legs and Daniel 9:26 and the people who destroyed the Temple. Where else do you think our whole theology on the end times might be challenged and might be changed in Scripture?"

"I guess in that light it could be anywhere," Joe confessed. "This new interpretation of Daniel 8 does place us in a unique position. I can see how if Daniel 2:40 and Daniel 9:26 change, there might be changes in our interpretations elsewhere."

"Right. And there is a consistent pattern of events across a few Bible passages, starting with Daniel 8. Remember, in Daniel 8 we saw five major events—five parts to the vision. First we saw the second horn of the ram grow up. Second, the ram invaded the Middle East—the Iranian invasion, which of course starts a major war. Third, we saw a goat with a single horn running back east and trampling the ram. This represents another country in the Middle East—a Sunni one—fighting back and destroying Iran.

"You mentioned it could be Turkey."

"Right," responded Mike. "And fourth we noted the four horns appear with a little horn growing out of one of them, which is another event, the Antichrist emerging and growing in power. Fifth, and finally, we saw the horn making war on the saints and stopping the sacrifice which happens during the Tribulation. So, there are four events and then the Tribulation. The Iranian invasion, which is the start of a great war, is the second event. A full discussion of these other passages could take hours, and it's getting late. Davidson in his book, *Daniel Revisited,* discusses all these passages and how they connect with one another. Just to touch on them, the passages are Daniel 7, Matthew 24:4–8, and Revelation 6:1–8."

"Daniel 7—the vision of the four beasts?" asked Joe.

"Yes. There are clues in Daniel 7 showing us there might be a parallel to Daniel 8. Daniel was under the last ruling king of Babylon when in Daniel 7:17 he tells us all four beasts are kings that *will* arise. Therefore, they all must rise *after* ancient Babylon. So the first beast, which is thought to be ancient Babylon, must be something later. Also, Daniel 7 shows us four beasts representing four events, and then the little horn comes up last. This is the Antichrist during the Tribulation again. Just as the ram runs out as the second event in Daniel 8, the bear in Daniel 7 is the second beast. Not only does the bear start a war by being commanded to eat other animals, but it is higher on one side just as the ram has a higher horn. Anyway, the bear gives us a clue that many nations will be consumed—presumably the nations west and south of Iran. This confirms for us that nations with the oil will be involved, and will be overwhelmed."

"I think my brain is on overload, I'll have to go back and reread these passages, but that's intriguing," said Joe.

"I know this is a lot to take in, so I'll keep it brief. The second passage is Matthew 24:4–8 where Jesus tells us about the birth pains prior to the Tribulation, and there are four birth pains."

"That's an interesting take on the birth pains," Joe said. "We all thought they had been going on for the last hundred years, but they might all be specific events right before the Tribulation."

"That's right—they could be. Anyway, the second birth pain is war. And Jesus gives us an ominous warning only for war. My NIV Bible says 'don't be alarmed.' But the Greek word used there in Matthew 24:6 is only used in two places in the whole New Testament. Scholars had to go to secular sources like Homer's *Iliad* to find out what it meant. The word doesn't mean just 'to be alarmed.' No, it means to *scream in terror*! Jesus is telling us to not scream in terror."

"That raises the intensity, for sure" said Joe. "I guess in addition to rereading several passages we need to pay more careful attention to the meanings of words we thought we didn't need to worry about."

"Apparently. Now the third and last passage is Revelation 6:1–8."

"Isn't that the four horsemen?" asked Joe, turning quickly to Revelation.

"Yes. The fifth seal in Revelation 6 reveals to us a picture from the Tribulation, with the martyrdom of the saints. But there are four seals prior to the fifth, releasing four horses with four events again prior to the Tribulation."

"There's that pattern of four again," Joe said.

"And here again we see the second horseman riding the red horse represents—"

"War!" Joe cut in, sounding surprised. "I never connected the dots before."

"Remember what is said about the second horseman. He not only has power to cause men to slay or butcher one another within the Middle East—which is war—but he has power to take peace of mind and stability from the whole earth."

"What makes you think he has power to have men kill each other *only* in the Middle East?" asked Joe.

"Revelation 6:8 says the horsemen only have power over a quarter of the earth. Get this, Islam covers a quarter of the earth. Davidson clearly shows this in *Daniel Revisited*. Also, the colors of the horses—white, red, black, and green—are the colors of Islam and the flags of Muslim nations."

"That's really interesting," said Joe.

"Look at this connection. The second horseman is also said to have power to take the peace of mind from the whole earth. This of course could easily be caused by Iran stopping the oil supply."

"Yes, that would be the reason. You see a pattern among these passages, don't you?"

"Well, yes," responded Joe. "Not only are there four events prior to the Tribulation as you were saying, but there seem to be warnings about war associated with the second event whether it's a ram, a horseman, a bear, or Jesus himself."

"Right."

"This bears some investigation," said Joe. "I can see that, in fact, Daniel 8 certainly seems to be showing us the grave consequence of Iran's action all by itself. We really don't need the other passages to tell us Iran could potentially impact the world very seriously. But, I admit, those other passages should be studied some more and might sway some skeptics. If they do apply, they are telling us that the potentially bad things to occur will, in fact, be part of our lives until the Tribulation. And it's the Bible telling us this."

Mike said, "That's right. And either way, whether from Scripture or from an analysis of what Iran's actions could result in, the oil prices and possible oil shortages will lead to a challenge for many of us as Christians."

"Yes," said Joe. "I've been thinking how easy it is for us in the West to be Christians in a rich country. But we must continue as light and salt in this world even in economic chaos. I don't know if our people are prepared for this."

Mike Branch looked at Pastor Joe and said, "They will need to be ready. It means going back to the basics and remembering what is most important—loving others, including doing good to our enemies. Witnessing includes these things as well as preaching the gospel. To effectively do this we must have a close relationship with Christ, surrendering all we are and all we have to Him."

"You've given me a lot to think and pray about, Mike."

EIGHT

THE WARNING

"Joe, we western Christians have another problem to overcome. Up to now we've all been armchair prophecy students. It's easy to do. The problem is we have to change our mindsets."

"What do you mean?"

"Up to now, studying prophecy was just an interesting collection of things to note, but it never really connected in a concrete and physical way to our lives. I think we studied prophecy for two reasons: the first was to try to figure out how close we are to Christ's return. And the second was just out of curiosity. Many of us wonder about the Antichrist—who will he be and what might he do? But I don't know if anyone really thought we'd be here to see hard times and experience the events witnessing the emergence of the Antichrist. Some think the Rapture is next and some think the return of Christ itself is next. In any case, fulfillment of end-time prophecy was seen as mostly being disconnected from our actual day to day lives."

"But now with this message . . ." Joe chimed in.

"With this message," Mike echoed and continued, "If this new interpretation is true, the prophetic landscape and how we relate to prophecy will change, possibly before, but more likely *after* Iran's invasion. Prophecy is now telling us about events that will affect us in our daily lives, events that will be in our faces and will be unavoidable—things that will change our lives in the years prior to the Rapture. Armchair prophecy speculation like we have been accustomed to will be replaced by in-your-face, empty-the-bank-account living and depending completely on the Lord for sustenance in these end times."

"Many of us have never lived like that," Joe said, shaking his head. "What's the bottom line here for Christians, Mike?"

"The first thing we must realize is what this invasion—and indeed all the events after that—truly means. When Iran invades there will likely be chaos in the world. Those who don't know the message will likely panic, and 'scream in terror.' Just what Jesus tells us not to do. When Jesus tells us in Scripture not to do something, it is usually because that is what we feel like doing."

"Isn't that the truth," said Joe.

"We must not get caught up in the chaos and let fear consume us. Most importantly, we must understand that when we see the invasion by Iran it is the next event foretold in Scripture being fulfilled—the next event foretold by Scripture that tells us Christ is indeed coming back!"

"I can see even Christians being overtaken by fear when that happens," said Joe.

"Right. Jesus may have been talking about this very event when He said don't scream in terror. That's why I felt it was so important for me to drive all this way to give you this message. When the invasion occurs, Christian lay people and pastors need to be able to show the world, using Scripture, that this terrible Iranian invasion and economic chaos is all about Christ's coming. That's the answer you must give your community."

"We have been preaching that for two thousand years!" said Joe.

"It's not good enough to simply say 'Christ is coming' when this chaos arrives. People will be very afraid. It needs to be shown that the very movement of Iranian troops across the Middle East is the next event leading up to Christ's return, and signaling it directly. This next event is just as real, and just as much a part of our Lord's return as the lightning flashing across the sky and heaven being ripped asunder as our Messiah appears in glory. For this invasion by Iran triggers the goat's charge, which sets up the scene for the Antichrist to emerge and grow in power. This leads in turn to the Tribulation, and finally Christ's return to earth to rule. And you can show much of this in Daniel 8. Instead of panicking and screaming like everyone else, you'll know plainly God is indeed in control. You will also know time is indeed short. With this knowledge you can continue to preach the gospel and win souls."

"I'm going to start preparing my people, so they will be ready as well," said Joe.

"By the way, remember how I said the goat mentioned in Daniel will likely be Turkey, leading three other Sunni nations. We will likely then witness the great nation created across the Middle East break into four pieces. Then the man who is to be the Antichrist will emerge from one of the four nations. He will then reconquer the nations to unite them. At least that's how I see Daniel 8. It's also explained in *Daniel Revisited*. And when all these things happen we will know the Tribulation is at the door. But, throughout the occurrences of all these terrible things, you, and I, and all pastors and believers, can continue to reach the lost with the gospel."

"This message is definitely a wake-up call for me. I need to show my flock how all these things will happen—and because God's Word says so."

"It's a wake-up call indeed for all of us, Joe. It's a time to prepare, know what's coming, and act on it. That's why this message was sealed until now. It wasn't needed until now. God knew just the time when this message was needed and is releasing it."

"Praise God for that, Mike!"

"Amen," Mike responded. "Well, I think we're done. I really do thank you for so graciously taking the time to listen."

"Well, thank-you for driving all the way out here to talk with me," said Pastor Taylor. "This has been life changing. I'm going to share this message with my people, and the group of area pastors I meet with."

NINE

---❖---

IN THE NEWS

As Mike Branch stood up to leave, he said, "I want to leave this with you." He pulled a copy of *Daniel Revisited* from his backpack and handed it to Joe.

"Thanks! I'll definitely read this."

Just then the two men heard the sound of quick footsteps in the hallway.

"Sorry to interrupt," said Sharon, the pastor's assistant as she knocked and then entered the pastor's office. She seemed tense and anxious. "You probably haven't heard—?"

"Heard what?" asked Joe.

"It looks like Iranian forces have started an invasion. It's on every news channel on the radio. News anchors are comparing it to the Iran-Iraq War when hundreds of thousands of young men came rushing over the borders from Iran into Iraq. Speculation is the Iranians are headed into Iraq towards ISIS, and into the Arabian Peninsula!"

"Oh, my Lord!" exclaimed Joe. "It's really happening." He turned and said, "Thanks, Sharon, I'll explain it all to you later."

The two men shook hands. Mike said, "Well, Joe, talk about timing. It's good you could hear the message before this happened."

"Looks like I have some phone calls to make," said the pastor. "What are you going to do? Can you stick around tonight?"

"No, unfortunately," answered Mike. "I have to get back home. There are several other pastors who will want to talk after hearing this news."

"Do you have enough gas for the drive?" asked Joe. "This might cause a panic for gas right now."

"Not a problem. I always keep the tank nearly full and filled it just before arriving. It's something I've been doing lately."

At the entrance to the church the two men said their good-byes.

"God bless you, Pastor Joe. I'll be in touch, as long as the phones and email still work," Mike said, smiling warmly.

"God bless you too. I won't forget this. If we don't see each other again I'll see you on that Day."

Mike Branch walked out the door into the night air. He looked up at the stars. *The world is changing*, he thought. *It's the end time. We are now on the road to the end of the age. Father, help me share the message of hope you've provided us with, and be a light to the world in the dark days to come.*

EPILOGUE

AN INVITATION

How about you? Can you believe this interpretation of Daniel 8? Can you see the truth of the warning? Do you see Iran positioning itself for such an invasion? If this event actually takes place, will you be ready, and be aware of what is truly happening? Will you be able to get over the surprise that the Rapture or Second Coming is not next—and that we will face some horrendous times?

If you haven't already, accept the Lord Jesus Christ as your Savior and surrender all you are and all you have to Him now. You will need his wisdom and direction in these dark times to come. Learn to depend on Him. Let Christ guide you.

There are ways to physically prepare for the hard times to come, but none of them will help unless you belong to Christ. You can store food, buy gold, buy foreign stocks, start a garden, and have guns and ammo, but these things cannot be your security. The living God of heaven must be your God—and your security. You must "dwell in the shelter of the Most High" to "rest in the shadow of the Almighty," as Psalm 91:1 says.

Father God, let your Word and your glory be displayed in these last days to the entire world. Let the church understand what is happening so she can be the light you want her to be. Help the church to focus on the task at hand—to preach the gospel and be a witness even through these terrible times shortly to come. Let brothers and sisters realize the end times are not about the awful things to happen—wars, chaos, and emerging Antichrist—but about the transition of the rule of this world to Jesus Christ, and the last act of our salvation into our new, glorious bodies so we can serve, worship, and commune with our Lord forever. In Jesus' name, Amen.

ENDNOTES

CHAPTER 2

1. Mark Davidson, *Daniel Revisited: Discovering the Four Mideast Signs Leading to the Antichrist* (Nashville: Thomas Nelson, 2016).
2. Ibid., 25–61.
3. Joel Richardson, *Mideast Beast: The Scriptural Case for an Islamic Antichrist* (Washington D.C.: WND Books, 2012).

CHAPTER 3

1. Robert Tait, "Iran to Rebuild Spectacular Tent City at Persepolis," *The Guardian*, Sept. 22, 2005, https://www.theguardian.com/world/2005/sep/22/arts.iran.

CHAPTER 4

1. Ali Alfoneh, *Iran Unveiled: How the Revolutionary Guards Is Turning Theocracy into Military Dictatorship* (Washington D.C.: AEI Press, 2013), 27.
2. Ibid., 165, 171.
3. Ibid., 175.
4. Ibid., 176.
5. Ali Alfoneh, "All the Guard's Men: Iran's Silent Revolution," *World Affairs*, September–October 2010, http://www.worldaffairsjournal.org/article/all-guards-men-irans-silent-revolution.
6. Jason Gewirtz, "Revolutionary Guard Has Tight Grip on Iran's Economy," CNBC, Dec. 8, 2010, http://www.cnbc.com/id/40570657.
7. Farnaz Fassihi, "Protests in Iran Diminish Amid Security Crackdown," *Wall Street Journal*, June 23, 2009, http://online.wsj.com/article/SB124566035538436595.html.
8. Alfoneh, *Iran Unveiled*, 246.

CHAPTER 5

1. Paul Bucala, and Frederick W. Kagan, "Iran's Evolving Way of War: How the IRGC Fights in Syria," *American Enterprise Institute*, March 24, 2016, http://www.irantracker.org/sites/default/files/imce-images/Irans_Evolving Way_of_War_IRGC_in_Syria_FINAL.pdf.
2. Christopher Harmer, "The Strategic Impact of the S-300 in Iran," Aug. 2016; *American Enterprise Institute*, http://www.irantracker.org/analysis/harmer-strategic-impact-s-300-iran-august-18-2016.

CHAPTER 6

1. Jean Calmard, "Ayatollah," *The Oxford Encyclopedia of the Islamic World*, accessed Oct. 23, 2015, http://www.oxfordislamicstudies.com/article/opr/t236/e0088.
2. Alfoneh, *Iran Unveiled*, 17.
3. Kasra Naji, *Ahmadinejad: The Secret History of Iran's Radical Leader* (Berkeley: University of California Press, 2008), 69.
4. Naji, *Ahmadinejad*, 69.
5. Mark Davidson, "Ahmadinejad's Speeches to the U.N.: Talks of the Second Signpost," *Four Signposts*, Oct. 8, 2012, http://foursignposts.com/2012/10/08/ahmadinejads-speeches-to-the-u-n-talks-of-the-second-signpost/.
6. Ibid.
7. Alfoneh, *Iran Unveiled*, 151.

CHAPTER 7

1. EIA Country Profiles: Japan; retrieved on Oct. 30, 2016; https://www.eia.gov/beta/international/analysis.cfm?iso=JPN.
2. U.S. Energy Information Administration, International Energy Statistics; http://www.eia.gov/beta/international/data/browser/#/?pa=00000000000000000000008&c=ruvvvvvfvtvnvvlurvvvvfv vvvvvfvvvou20evvvvvvvvvvnvvuvo&ct=0&tl_id=5-A&vs=INTL.5 7-6-AFG-BB.A&ord=SA&cy=2014&vo=0&v=H&start=1980.

TEXT OF DANIEL 8 (NIV 1984)

[1] In the third year of King Belshazzar's reign, I, Daniel, had a vision, after the one that had already appeared to me. [2] In my vision I saw myself in the citadel of Susa in the province of Elam; in the vision I was beside the Ulai Canal. [3] I looked up, and there before me was a ram with two horns, standing beside the canal, and the horns were long. One of the horns was longer than the other but grew up later. [4] I watched the ram as he charged toward the west and the north and the south. No animal could stand against him, and none could rescue from his power. He did as he pleased and became great.

[5] As I was thinking about this, suddenly a goat with a prominent horn between his eyes came from the west, crossing the whole earth without touching the ground. [6] He came toward the two-horned ram I had seen standing beside the canal and charged at him in great rage. [7] I saw him attack the ram furiously, striking the ram and shattering his two horns. The ram was powerless to stand against him; the goat knocked him to the ground and trampled on him, and none could rescue the ram from his power. [8] The goat became very great, but at the height of his power his large horn was broken off, and in its place four prominent horns grew up toward the four winds of heaven.

[9] Out of one of them came another horn, which started small but grew in power to the south and to the east and toward the Beautiful Land. [10] It grew until it reached the host of the heavens, and it threw some

of the starry host down to the earth and trampled on them. [11] It set itself up to be as great as the Prince of the host; it took away the daily sacrifice from him, and the place of his sanctuary was brought low. [12] Because of rebellion, the host of the saints and the daily sacrifice were given over to it. It prospered in everything it did, and truth was thrown to the ground.

[13] Then I heard a holy one speaking, and another holy one said to him, "How long will it take for the vision to be fulfilled-the vision concerning the daily sacrifice, the rebellion that causes desolation, and the surrender of the sanctuary and of the host that will be trampled underfoot?"

[14] He said to me, "It will take 2,300 evenings and mornings; then the sanctuary will be reconsecrated."

[15] While I, Daniel, was watching the vision and trying to understand it, there before me stood one who looked like a man. [16] And I heard a man's voice from the Ulai calling, "Gabriel, tell this man the meaning of the vision."

[17] As he came near the place where I was standing, I was terrified and fell prostrate. "Son of man," he said to me, "understand that the vision concerns the time of the end."

[18] While he was speaking to me, I was in a deep sleep, with my face to the ground. Then he touched me and raised me to my feet.

[19] He said: "I am going to tell you what will happen later in the time of wrath, because the vision concerns the appointed time of the end. [20] The two-horned ram that you saw represents the kings of Media and Persia. [21] The shaggy goat is the king of Greece, and the large horn between his eyes is the first king. [22] The four horns that replaced the one that was broken off represent four kingdoms that will emerge from his nation but will not have the same power.

[23] "In the latter part of their reign, when rebels have become completely wicked, a stern-faced king, a master of intrigue, will arise. [24] He will become very strong, but not by his own power. He will cause astounding devastation and will succeed in whatever he does. He will destroy the mighty men and the holy people. [25] He will cause deceit to prosper, and he will consider himself superior. When they feel secure, he will destroy many and take his stand against the Prince of princes. Yet he will be destroyed, but not by human power.

[26] "The vision of the evenings and mornings that has been given you is true, but seal up the vision, for it concerns the distant future."

[27] I, Daniel, was exhausted and lay ill for several days. Then I got up and went about the king's business. I was appalled by the vision; it was beyond understanding.

ABOUT THE AUTHOR

Mark Davidson is the author of *Daniel Revisited*, published by Thomas Nelson, and he is a follower of Jesus Christ. Being a lifelong student of the Bible, eschatology, world history, and geopolitics, he has connected the dots, yielding a new interpretation of Daniel that is being proven by current events. Mark has a graduate degree in aerospace engineering, having worked over thirty years in the defense and space industries, and he and his wife live in Colorado.

For more information, please visit www.foursignposts.com.